JBIOG
Adele
Tieck, Sara

Adele

Adele

ABDO Publishing Company

by **Sarah Tieck**

Big Buddy BOOKS
Buddy Bios

 PRINTED ON RECYCLED PAPER

Coordinating Series Editor: Rochelle Baltzer
Contributing Editors: Megan M. Gunderson, Marcia Zappa
Graphic Design: Maria Hosley
Cover Photograph: *Getty Images*: Jon Kopaloff/FilmMagic.
Interior Photographs/Illustrations: *AP Photo*: John Marshall,JME (p. 7), Chris Pizzello (p. 29), PRNewsFoto/RCA
     Records (p. 13), Rex Features via AP Images (pp. 14, 15), Joel Ryan,file (pp. 5, 15), Matt Sayles,file (pp. 11, 21,
     25), Mike Stephens (p. 11), Mark J. Terrill (p. 21); *Getty Images*: Dave Etheridge-Barnes (p. 17), Jo Hale (p. 13),
     Marl Holloway (18), Stacie McChesney/NBC/NBCU Photo Bank via Getty Images (p. 27), Donna Ward (p. 23);
     Shutterstock: S. Borisov (p. 9).

Cataloging-in-Publication Data

Tieck, Sarah.
  Adele: singing sensation / Sarah Tieck.
     p. cm. -- (Big buddy biographies)
  ISBN 978-1-61783-747-0
  1. Adele, 1988- --Juvenile literature. 2. Singers--England--Biography--Juvenile literature.   I. Title.
  782.42164092--dc22
  [B]
                         2012946534

Contents

Rising Star

Adele is a talented singer. She sings and writes popular music. She is best known for her strong, deep singing voice. Fans around the world love her albums and songs!

Where in the World?

Scotland

NORTH SEA

Northern
Ireland

UNITED
KINGDOM

ATLANTIC
OCEAN

IRELAND

Wales

England
London

Family Ties

Adele's full name is Adele Laurie Blue Adkins. She was born in Tottenham, London, England, on May 5, 1988.

Adele's parents are Penny Adkins and Mark Evans. Adele has a younger half brother named Cameron.

Adele has thanked her mom for helping her become a successful singer.

Did you know...

Adele's father chose the middle name Blue. He picked it because he loved blues music.

7

Growing Up

When Adele was about three years old, her parents split up. After this, Adele didn't see her dad very often. She lived with her mom in apartments around London. Adele's mom had many jobs. These included a furniture maker and an office worker.

London is a large city located on the river Thames. It has many famous sites, such as the Big Ben clock tower.

Adele listened to music from a young age. She went to her first concert at age three. As Adele grew up, she listened to different types of music. This is how she taught herself to sing.

As a girl, Adele listened to popular music. She especially enjoyed the Spice Girls (*above*).

Talented Singers

Adele has learned a lot from singers of the past. Some of her favorites are Etta James, Roberta Flack, and Ella Fitzgerald. They are known for **rhythm and blues**, **soul**, and **jazz** music.

Adele uses these music styles when she sings. She is especially known for her deep, soulful voice. She writes songs about her life and feelings.

After hearing American rhythm and blues singer Etta
James (*above*), Adele knew she wanted to be a singer.

Becoming an Artist

Adele hoped to become a music artist. She wanted to write and sing her own songs. Around 2002, Adele was accepted at the BRIT School for Performing Arts and Technology. There, she learned more about becoming a singer.

Other well-known singers also attended BRIT. Some include Jessie J (*left*), Leona Lewis (*below*), and Amy Winehouse (*right*).

Adele uses the skills she learned at BRIT to perform as a singer.

For one of her BRIT classes, Adele had to record music. She shared her **demo** with a friend. The songs were so good that Adele's friend put them online.

Soon, many people noticed Adele's singing talent. Then in 2006, Adele **graduated** from high school.

Adele has a larger body size than many other popular singers. So when she became famous, some people said she should lose weight. But, Adele said she was happy with her size and shape.

Big Break

A few months after graduating, Adele made a deal with a recording company. She worked hard to record her first album. She wrote and sang many songs for it. Her debut album was released in 2008. It is called *19*.

Before the album came out, the song "Hometown Glory" was released. "Chasing Pavements" was also released early. It became a hit!

Singing Star

In 2009, Adele won awards for *19*. She won **Grammy Awards** for "Chasing Pavements" and for being a new artist. People wondered if Adele's next songs would be as good.

In 2010, Adele **released** a new song called "Rolling in the Deep." It became a hit right away! People were excited for Adele's new album, *21*. It came out in 2011.

After winning two Grammy Awards in 2009, Adele was excited to win again in 2012. She won six Grammys for her work on *21*!

A Musical Life

Adele spends many hours writing and recording music. She also practices singing before **performing**.

When she is on tour, Adele may spend months away from home. She travels to cities around the world and performs live concerts.

Adele attends events and meets fans. Her fans are always excited to see her!

23

In 2011, Adele had some trouble with her voice. Because of this, she had to have throat surgery.

To give her body time to heal, Adele stopped singing and doing concerts. Fans were disappointed. But, Adele didn't want to hurt her singing voice. She healed and was able to **perform** again in 2012.

Off the Stage

Adele is a mother. She spends free time at home with her friends and family in London. They enjoy playing games and watching TV.

Adele also likes to work with groups that help people in need. Sometimes, she **performs** at events to raise money for special causes.

Adele travels to talk to reporters and television hosts. She has appeared on *Last Call with Carson Daly*.

Reporters often take Adele's picture. And, fans ask for her autograph.

Buzz

Adele's opportunities continue to grow. In 2012, she took time off from recording and touring to grow her family and heal her throat. But, she kept writing songs and planning her next album. Fans are excited to see what she'll sing next!

Did you know...

Adele's music has been used in television shows and movies.

Snapshot

★**Name**: Adele Laurie Blue Adkins

★**Birthday**: May 5, 1988

★**Birthplace**: Tottenham, London, England

★**Albums**: *19, 21*

Important Words

debut (DAY-byoo) a first appearance.

demo a recording to show a musical group or artist's abilities.

graduate (GRA-juh-wayt) to complete a level of schooling.

Grammy Award any of the awards given each year by the National Academy of Recording Arts and Sciences. Grammy Awards honor the year's best accomplishments in music.

jazz a form of American music that features lively and unusual beats. It first became popular in the early 1900s.

perform to do something in front of an audience.

release to make available to the public.

rhythm (RIH-thuhm) **and blues** a form of popular music that features a strong beat. It is inspired by jazz, gospel, and blues styles.

soul a form of African-American music. It expresses deep feeling and includes gospel and rhythm and blues styles.

Web Sites

To learn more about Adele, visit ABDO Publishing Company online. Web sites about Adele are featured on our Book Links page. These links are routinely monitored and updated to provide the most current information available.

www.abdopublishing.com

Index